Jetliner GLORY

Jetliner GLORY

Airliner Liveries

JOHN K. MORTON

Motorbooks International
Publishers & Wholesalers ®

Contents

This edition first published in 1997 by Motorbooks International, Publishers & Wholesalers, 729 Prospect Avenue, PO Box 1, Osceola, WI 54020, USA.

© John K. Morton

Previously published by Airlife Publishing Ltd, Shrewsbury, England.

Library of Congress Cataloging-in-Publication Data available

ISBN 0-7603–0515–3

Printed and bound in Singapore.

Introduction

Welcome to *Jetliner Glory* where I invite you to take a look at a further selection of colour schemes from airlines all over the world. All the pictures contained in this volume have been taken by myself and selected from my rapidly expanding collection of 22,000 slides. It would be quite impossible to include examples of every airline's colour scheme in a book of this size, however, it is hoped that the selection contained herein, together with those in my earlier book *Flying Colours*, will provide the reader with the information they may be looking for. The book is intended to cover the world as far as is practicable, commencing in Europe and then following an easterly route ending in the USA and Canada, including as many carriers as pages will allow.

In obtaining the majority of the pictures in this book, I was fortunate to be given the help and assistance of several airline executives, and many airport employees both on the ground and in administrative positions at the airports I visited. I am extremely grateful to these individuals, without whose help and patience many of the pictures could not have been obtained.

John K. Morton

Chapter 1
Europe

Icelandair was established in 1973 as the Icelandic flag-carrier, operating scheduled and charter passenger and cargo services from its Reykjavik base. As well as providing services to destinations within Iceland, the carrier serves cities in Europe, the Mediterranean and the USA. Icelandair's fleet comprises Fokker 50s, which are used on short internal services, and Boeing 737 and 757 twin-jets, providing services to more distant destinations. Photographed on approach to London Heathrow in July 1996 is Boeing 757 TF-FIK, then their latest 757 to be delivered to the airline, having entered service in March of the same year. This is a non-stop service from Reykjavik and the airliner is scheduled to remain on the ground for one hour before commencing its return flight.

Air Atlanta Lockheed L1011 TriStar TF-ABL performed as a stand-by aircraft for the United Kingdom airline Britannia during the summer months of 1995, being based at Manchester and put into service as and when necessary. This enabled Britannia to meet all their flight requirements and keep to their planned schedule even if unforeseen delays occurred which made their regular aircraft unavailable. Air Atlanta acquired the L1011 in May 1995 and its colours identify the aircraft as originally being in Cathay Pacific's fleet. When photographed in September 1995, Alpha-Bravo-Lima was carrying holidaymakers from Manchester and was about to touch-down at Palma.

Air Atlanta Icelandic, based in Iceland, was established in 1986 and specialises in wet-leased scheduled operations for national carriers. In May 1993 the airline also entered the charter market which continued to operate alongside their national leasing programme. Boeing 737 series 300 TF-ABK is seen operating flights on behalf of the Portuguese company Aviareps, and was photographed in September 1995 about to land on the island of Majorca.

All Leisure Airlines operated Airbus Industrie A320 aircraft, leasing as required from Dublin-based Translift Airways. Two of the A320s received the full colour scheme of All Leisure, and were based in the United Kingdom during the summer of 1995 to provide charter flights to the popular sun destinations in Europe. Regular flights from and to Manchester were made during this time. It is at this city's Terminal 2 that EI-TLH was photographed at the start of the package holiday season in May 1995 being pushed back from the gate at the commencement of its journey to a Mediterranean sun-spot.

Regional and domestic airline Ryanair was established in 1985 as an independent Irish carrier. Based in Dublin, the carrier currently has a fleet of eleven Boeing 737 series 200 aircraft all of them being configured economy class with 130 seats. The Ryanair livery seen on Boeing 737 EI-CJI at Manchester in June 1994 was introduced at the beginning of 1992 and supersedes that originally carried on the airline's BAC 1-11s. A slight modification to the scheme was made in the spring of 1995 when billboard-style titles appeared on the fuselage of a 737. The Boeing in question is EI-CKS which was also photographed at the Lancashire city whilst operating the Dublin–Manchester service in July 1996.

Air UK was formed in January 1980 by the merger of four airlines from the United Kingdom: Air Anglia, Air Wales, Air Westwood and British Island Airways. The company is based at Stansted, the East Anglian airport, from where the airline's fleet of Fokker 27s, Fokker 100s and BAe 146s provide both regional and European services. The airline was the first in Europe to put BAe 146 series 300 models into service, which replaced the earlier series 200 model. The present livery was introduced to coincide with the delivery of their first BAe 146 at the end of 1987 and is shown applied to Fokker 100 G-UKFH about to return to England from Amsterdam Schiphol on a late evening flight in April 1995.

British Midland is a well known and respected United Kingdom domestic and charter airline, having gained several awards including Best UK Domestic and Best Short Haul carrier to quote but a few. Founded in 1938 and originally known as Derby Airways, the airline moved to its present base at East Midlands Airport in 1964, and during that year changed its title to British Midland Airways. It was not until 1970 that the carrier entered the jet age when BAC 1-11s began to operate their charter services, later to be joined by Boeing 707s which carried the original British Midland livery to American destinations on charter flights. The present attractive livery of the airline was introduced in 1985 and is seen on Boeing 737 series 500 G-BVKD approaching its allocated gate at Amsterdam's Schiphol airport in April 1995.

Air UK Leisure is a sister company of Air UK and was created in 1987 to provide charter flights to vacation destinations. The airline had its own dedicated fleet of Boeing 737 series 400s and the first flight in their charter programme occurred in early 1988. These airliners have since been taken out of the fleet and replaced by Airbus Industrie A320s. A sister company of Air UK Leisure is Leisure International Airways, which was founded in 1992 and currently operates two extended range Boeing 767s from London Gatwick and Manchester airports. This airline was formed to operate flights on behalf of tour company Unijet, a UK travel agency. The leased airliners entered service on regular transatlantic routes to Orlando and Montego Bay, and G-UKLH, photographed on push-back at Manchester in May 1995, is about to commence one of these services.

Following the demise of the United Kingdom airline Ambassador, Air Foyle founded Sabre Airways in 1994 and repainted the failed airline's Boeing 737s in the colours of the newly-formed company. Boeing 727s, formerly flying in Dan Air colours, also joined the Sabre fleet which currently consists of two 727s and two 737s. Based at London Gatwick, the airline began operations from various British regional airports providing charter flights to the main European holiday destinations. Boeing 727 G-BNNI remained stored following the collapse of Dan Air until joining Sabre and being repainted in the colours of its new owner. The tri-jet was overnighting at Manchester airport when photographed in May 1995.

(Previous page)
British Mediterranean Airways commenced operations at the end of October 1994 with flights from London Heathrow, its main base and hub, to the Lebanese capital city, Beirut. Since the introduction of this service, the airline continues to provide direct non-stop flights to Beirut with continuing services on certain days to the Jordanian capital, Amman, and Syrian capital, Damascus. The company still has the one aircraft with which services were started, a leased Airbus Industrie A320, G-MEDA, illustrated here about to land at Heathrow in July 1996 after completing the journey from Damascus.

Manchester Terminal 1 is the location for this picture of Boeing 757 G-RJGR, seen approaching its gate in June 1995 after returning from a Spanish destination with a complement of holidaymakers. Airtours International is part of the United Kingdom Airtours Group and operates the group's charter flights with a fleet of Airbus and Boeing airliners. The company's new livery, seen here on Golf-Romeo, was introduced in January 1995; the red, green and yellow logo on the tail is that of travel agency Going Places, a chain owned by the Airtours group.

In order to launch a new twice-weekly London–Hong Kong–Taipei service in March 1993, it was necessary for British Airways to modify their basic livery so as not to carry any flags or national insignia. This was due to the UK government only recognising Taiwan as a province of the Republic of China. As a result, Boeing 747 series 400 G-BNLZ received British Asia Airways titles with Chinese characters on the tail and was then used exclusively on this route. The aircraft made a surprise visit to Miami in December 1995 and was photographed about to land after being put into service on the daily flight from London Heathrow.

Airworld Aviation Limited, a British inclusive charter airline owned by the Thomas Cook Group, is a sister company of Sunworld, and was started in 1994 to guarantee availability of aircraft seats for Sunworld's inclusive tours from points in the UK to the Mediterranean resorts. The airline operates from April through to October with a fleet of leased Airbus Industrie A320s and A321s, the first example of the latter type entering service at the commencement of the airline's 1997 season. During the 1994/5 and 1995/6 winters the three A320s in Airworld's fleet provided services from Canadian cities after being re-registered into the Canadian register. Spanish destinations are very popular with the British holidaymaker with the island of Majorca being one of the major sun-spots, and it is at this island's Palma airport that Airbus A320 G-BVZU was photographed in June 1995 upon its arrival on a Saturday flight from Manchester.

The charter airline Flightline was established in 1989 and flies to the European resorts during the summer months and the ski resorts in winter from its bases in Southend and Stansted in the south of England. There are currently six aircraft in the fleet including three British Aerospace BAe 146s. G-BPNT is their only 300 series model which is sub-leased and operated for Palmair, a division of Flightline. When photographed in September 1995, the airliner was awaiting clearance from the Palma tower for its return to the UK.

Originally formed to operate services on behalf of British Airtours and the charter operations of British Caledonian Airways, Caledonian Airways is no longer a subsidiary of British Airways and is now an international charter airline operating on behalf of its parent company, Inspirations, a United Kingdom tour company. Based at London Gatwick, the airline's fleet of Airbus Industrie A320s, Lockheed TriStar L1011s and a McDonnell Douglas DC-10 provide services to European, Caribbean and North American destinations. Caledonian's first A320 was delivered in the spring of 1995, and the second example to enter service was G-BVYB, which was photographed in November of that year being pushed back from its Manchester gate at the start of a flight to a Mediterranean destination.

EBA – Eurobelgian Airlines – commenced operations in April 1992 as an international charter and scheduled carrier. From its main base at Brussels, services to various European destinations are provided using their fleet of 300 and 400 series Boeing 737s. A proportion of the airline's business is transporting holidaymakers to the Spanish and other Mediterranean sunspots, whilst a twice-daily round-trip scheduled service operates between the cities of Brussels and Barcelona. Arriving at this Spanish city in June 1996 is OO-LTU, one of EBA's 300 models, which was the aircraft selected to operate the carrier's first flight on that day. The schedule allows only a 45-minute turn-around before the return to Belgium.

ChallengAir commenced flying in June 1994 as a non-scheduled charter passenger airline operating from its Brussels base providing extra capacity for travel organisations by leasing out their McDonnell Douglas DC-10 aircraft. The French airline Corsair found it necessary to lease additional aircraft for a short period at the start of the 1996 holiday season, and one of ChallengAir's DC-10s was acquired for a period of about three months. Whilst the full Corsair colours were not applied to the airliner for the duration of the lease, Corsair titles appeared together with ChallengAir's own titles on the fuselage as seen in the picture of OO-JOT about to depart from Manchester airport in June 1996.

Airbus Industrie A310 F-RADB is a VIP aircraft flying on behalf of the French government, and was making a scheduled stop at Palma airport when photographed in September 1995 after transporting ministers to an EEC meeting held on the island of Majorca. The aircraft is one of two of the type employed on government duties, and originally flew for Royal Jordanian Airlines in the colours of that carrier. It is illustrated in this state in my earlier book *Flying Colours*, published by Airlife in 1994, and at that time the A310 carried the registration F-ODVE and was named *Princess Iman*.

Air France is that country's national airline with a comprehensive route system operating from the Paris airports of Charles de Gaulle and Orly. With a staff of around 40,000 and a fleet of over 200 aircraft, Air France fly to over 160 worldwide destinations. The airline is part of the Groupe Air France, which also includes two other airlines: Air Charter and Air Inter. In 1993,

Air France was amongst the first of the world's carriers to put the Airbus Industrie A340 into passenger service and in December 1994, F-GNIE, one of eighteen A340s carrying Air France colours, was photographed about to touchdown at Miami airport arriving on a scheduled flight from Paris.

Established in 1958 as Martin's Air Charter, the present title Martinair was adopted in 1974. From its Amsterdam base, this Dutch international scheduled and charter passenger and cargo carrier operates a modern fleet of Airbus Industrie, Boeing and McDonnell Douglas airliners to destinations in the Americas, the Far East and Europe. One of Martinair's North American scheduled services is a regular 747 or MD-11 non-stop flight from Amsterdam to Miami. In December 1994 one of their Boeing 747s was put into service on the route and PH-MCE was photographed on finals to the Florida city.

Transavia, the Dutch charter and scheduled carrier, again revised its livery and launched a new image at the beginning of 1995 when one of their Boeing 737s appeared in yet another variation of the airline's basic green colour. Transavia's hub is at Amsterdam's Schiphol airport from where its fleet of Boeing 737s and 757s operate on services to London, Greece, Malta and holiday destinations in Spain. Boeing 757 PH-TKC had just recently acquired its new paint job when photographed taxying away from its Schiphol gate in April 1995.

Founded in The Hague in 1919, KLM today flies to 81 countries and 157 cities throughout the world from its Amsterdam Schiphol base. As the national airline of The Netherlands, KLM Royal Dutch Airlines is the oldest operating airline in the world and currently employs a staff in excess of 26,000. Their very impressive all-jet fleet, comprising examples from all the major manufacturers, provides the majority of the airline's services, whilst KLM Cityhopper, a subsidiary of KLM, provides regional services with a dedicated fleet of Saab and Fokker aircraft. McDonnell Douglas MD-11 trijets, which joined the KLM fleet in 1994, are used on services to North and South America, and Africa. Being prepared for one such duty at Schiphol in April 1995 is PH-KCD, the airline's fourth MD-11 to be delivered.

The new two-tone green livery of Germania was introduced by the German charter company in early 1992, replacing a similar colour scheme previously in use. Germania is a Cologne- and Berlin-based airline established in 1978 and was previously known as SAT. The change of name occurred in 1987, and at that time the airline updated their original fleet of Caravelles and Boeing 727s with newer Boeing 737s. Illustrated is D-AGEF, a 300 series 737, a type and model that is now flown exclusively by the carrier, and was photographed in September 1995 about to land at Palma with a complement of German tourists aboard.

Hapag-Lloyd is a major German charter airline operating from a base in Hannover with a large fleet of Boeing and Airbus Industrie passenger-carrying airliners, all of which are economy class-configured. Founded in 1972, its original fleet has since been completely replaced and it now has a fleet of totally leased aircraft, none being more than eight years old, which are regularly used on charter flights to various popular holiday destinations. Airbus A310 D-AHLX is a 264-seat, 1988-built airliner, one of eight such models in the Hapag-Lloyd fleet. This particular A310 is one of four in the company colours that have winglets and is seen taxying for take-off at Palma in September 1995.

Boeing 737 series 400 LX-LGG is the second of the type to be delivered to Luxair, the national airline of Luxembourg. The airline was established in 1961 and was previously known as Luxembourg Airlines until being renamed Luxair in 1962. Scheduled services are provided along with charter and inclusive tour flights utilising their fleet of Fokker and Boeing aircraft. The airliner illustrated was delivered new from Boeing, Luxair putting it into service in 1992, and was photographed at Palma in September 1995 shortly after vacating its stand.

Premiair was formed on 1 January 1994 by the merger of the Scandinavian airlines Conair of Denmark and Scanair of Sweden. Now based at Copenhagen airport, the airline operates international and regional charter services with a fleet of Airbus Industrie A300s/A320s and McDonnell Douglas DC-10s. From the Scandinavian airports of Copenhagen, Oslo and Stockholm, Premiair provides charter flights on behalf of tour companies to destinations within Europe. Operating such a flight in September 1995 is McDonnell Douglas DC-10 OY-CNT photographed as it arrives on a weekly service to Palma, Majorca.

The Swedish airline Sunways currently operates a fleet of three leased Boeing 757s from their Stockholm base. Founded in 1994, their first flight was made in May of the following year, and the airline now includes the United Kingdom and Spain in their extensive route network from various Scandinavian airports. Sunways operates charter flights on behalf of tour companies and in the summer of 1996 provided weekly direct charters from the two Turkish airports of Antalya and Izmir to the United Kingdom on behalf of the tour company Intersun with whom the airline has an alliance. It was possible to observe two of Sunways' 757s within 30 minutes of each other at Manchester airport on Mondays during the period of operation, and SE-DSM was photographed arriving at the airport's Terminal 2 in May 1996 just ahead of the second flight of the day.

Nordic East Airways has its main base at Stockholm's Arlanda airport from where international domestic scheduled and charter services are provided to destinations in Europe, the Middle East and North Africa. The airline commenced operations in 1991 when a McDonnell Douglas DC-9 leased from SAS was put into service on domestic routes out of Stockholm. The airline now has a fleet of two Boeing 737 series 300 and 400, and two Lockheed TriStar L1011 widebody aircraft in the fleet, and their 300 series 737 SE-DLO, was photographed at Frankfurt/Main in August 1995, about to depart.

TAP – Air Portugal – is the national carrier of Portugal, being formed as Transportes Aereas Portugueses in 1945. International and domestic scheduled passenger and freight services are provided which utilise their all-jet fleet of Boeing, Lockheed and Airbus Industrie airliners. The carrier's current livery was introduced in the early 1980s and is illustrated on one of their TriStar L1011s, CS-TED, photographed in August 1993 arriving at Frankfurt/Main. This airliner has carried the TAP colours since entering service when delivered new in 1983.

Futura International Airways was established in 1988 and commenced operations at the beginning of 1990 providing charter flights to Russia and countries within Europe from its main base on the Balearic island of Majorca. The carrier's entire fleet now consists of Boeing 737 series 400, 170-seat leased airliners all of which carry the very colourful Futura livery. EC-ETB, photographed about to land at the airliner's base in September 1995, was the first 737/400 aircraft to be put into traffic for Futura, having joined the airline in February 1990.

Air Europa Boeing 757 EC-FEF is part of a fleet of eighteen Boeings operated by this Spanish international charter company. The airline is based at Palma and operates to other Spanish islands and mainland along with European destinations in the UK, Germany and Holland. Long haul services include the Far East and the Americas. Air Europa's colours are identical to that of the now defunct UK airline Air Europe which folded in March 1991, the only difference being the use of lower case characters for the title instead of capitals. A variety of other carriers' aircraft can be seen at the terminal in the background as the 757 catches the early evening sun as it turns on to the runway after a sudden downpour.

The Spanish island of Majorca is one of Europe's main holiday destinations with visitors from most of the western European towns and cities selecting the resort due to its guaranteed good weather. The island's airport currently handles 14 million passengers a year, the majority of which pass through during the peak summer period of May through to October. A new terminal is in the course of construction to accommodate the expected increase in passengers, the first phase of which opened in April 1997. A small selection of carriers operating charter services in the summer of 1995 are illustrated in this spread, the first picture (top left) shows BAC 1-11 G-AVML in the colours of the UK airline European about to enter the runway for take-off. This air charter company based in the south of England resort of Bournemouth has a fleet consisting entirely of twenty 1-11 twin-jets which entered service with the carrier upon its formation in 1993.

Constellation operated its first flight in July 1995 and is currently flying two Boeing 727s which were previously in the fleet of the French airline Air Charter. Constellation's headquarters are in the Belgian capital Brussels, and during the summer of 1995 their 727s were based at Brussels and Palma, operating holiday charter flights. The colours shown on Boeing 727 F-GCMV still bore traces of the previous owner when photographed at Palma whilst being prepared to receive passengers.

35

Swiss charter airline Balair was formed in 1978 as a partly-owned subsidiary of Swissair, the national airline of Switzerland. In 1993, Balair merged with CTA (Compagnie de Transport Aérien), one of Swissair's subsidiaries, to become known as Balair CTA, and the company's aircraft began to appear with dual titles. The airline currently provides charter services to the Mediterranean and destinations in Europe and North America with a fleet of McDonnell Douglas DC-9s and Airbus Industrie A310s. The new livery of Balair introduced in 1992 shows a dark blue underside with yellow wings together with the usual red and white tail normally seen on Swiss aircraft. Airbus A310 HB-IPM was photographed in September 1995 arriving at Palma.

Alitalia is the national flag-carrying airline of Italy, being formed in 1946 as Aero Italiane Internazionali, a name it retained until 1957 when its present title was adopted. Its fleet of McDonnell Douglas, Airbus Industrie and Boeing aircraft are used on scheduled passenger and cargo services from its bases in Milan and Rome. The present livery was introduced in 1970 and is still in use today after a quarter of a century. Rome to Miami is one of Alitalia's long haul routes, and it is at Miami that Boeing 747 I-DEMN is seen about to land in December 1995.

Tarom, the airline of Romania, commenced operations in 1954 and has a mix of both Western- and Eastern-built airliners in its fleet. It is the largest airline in the country, providing both domestic and international scheduled passenger and cargo services. Tarom's main base is at Bucharest from where comprehensive services to many European cities are made. Other countries served include Africa, Asia and the Middle East, and Tarom recently commenced flights to New York and Chicago, with flights to North America being performed by extended-range Airbus Industrie A310s. On days when the airline's A310s are not operating over the north Atlantic, they are quite often put into service on flights to London Heathrow, and YR-LCA, named *Transilvania*, was operating such a service on a sunny Saturday when photographed in July 1996 at the end of its journey from Bucharest.

Adria, the Yugoslavian airline founded in 1961 as Adria Aviopproment, commenced charter operations with a small fleet of Douglas DC-6s, and later increased their services to include scheduled flights to various European cities. This name was retained by the airline until 1968 when the company was reorganised as part of the Inter Export Group, and the name changed to Inex Adria Airways. A further change occurred in May 1986 when the airline became independent, and the name Adria began to re-appear on the sides of the carrier's fleet of aircraft. The company is based in the Slovenia city Ljubljana, from where its fleet of McDonnell Douglas and Airbus Industrie airliners serve various European destinations. Airbus A320 S5-AAB illustrates the current colours of Adria and the European-built twin-jet was photographed in September 1995 soon after landing at Frankfurt/Main.

Eurocypria Airlines commenced operations in March 1992 and has its main bases at the Greek-Cypriot airports of Larnaca and Paphos. The airline is wholly-owned by Cyprus Airways and provides both passenger and cargo services with a fleet of three Airbus Industrie A320s leased from its parent company. The airliners carry the full colours of Eurocypria, and one example currently flown, 5B-DBB named *AKAMAS*, was photographed at its Manchester Terminal 2 gate on a very cold but brilliant 26 December 1993 whilst being prepared for its return to the island of Cyprus.

(Left top)
Cyprus Airways is a scheduled and charter passenger and cargo-carrying airline founded in 1947 by British European Airways and the government of Cyprus, the majority shareholding now being held by the Cyprus government. Based in Larnaca the airline's fleet consists entirely of Airbus Industrie A310 and A320 aircraft, all having entered service since 1989. The Middle East is prominent in the routeing structure although some of the main European cities are also included in the routes. The present Cyprus Airlines colours were introduced shortly after the airline disposed of its previous fleet of BAC 1-11s and Boeing 707s, and is carried on Airbus A320 5B-DAV, photographed whilst parked at Dubai International Airport in April 1994.

(Left bottom)
Birgenair is a Turkish international and regional charter airline based at Istanbul. The carrier was established in 1988 and during the summer months operates mainly to European destinations with a fleet of Boeing 737, 757 and 767 airliners. Photographed upon its arrival at Palma airport in June 1995 is TC-ASK, Birgenair's only 767 and an extended-range model. During Europe's quiet winter periods, this aircraft is often employed on flights to the Caribbean Islands, operating on behalf of tour companies.

Olympic Airways is the national airline of Greece, owned by the government of the country. Its main hub is at the capital city, Athens, from where international and regional services are provided utilising an all-jet fleet from the Boeing and Airbus factories, which take the Olympic colours to most countries of the world. North America is amongst the countries served, and a daily 747 flight to New York is provided. It is at this city's John F Kennedy airport that SX-OAD was photographed in May 1993 slowly making its way to the terminal. After about 90 minutes on the ground, *Olympic Flame* will leave on an overnight flight returning to Athens.

Kibris Turkish Airlines was previously
known as Cyprus Turkish Airlines, a
Nicosia-based scheduled and charter passenger airline. The carrier commenced
operations in February 1975, flights being
operated with aircraft leased from Turkish
Airlines as required. There are currently
four aircraft in the fleet of Kibris Turkish
Airlines at this time: three Boeing 727s and
one Airbus Industrie A310 which is leased
from Air France. This 225-seat economy
class airliner joined the Turkish airline at
the end of 1994 and is a frequent visitor to
London's Heathrow airport where TC-JYK
was photographed on a Saturday in July
1996.

Chapter 2

The Confederation of Independent States

From one beautiful paint job to another! Airbus Industrie A310 F-OGQZ previously carried the registration HC-BRB and the stylish and flamboyant bright colours of the South American airline Ecuatoriana. Upon the demise of this Ecuador-based airline, this aircraft, together with sister ship HC-BRA, returned to the leasing company to be re-leased to the Tashkent-based airline Uzbekistan, appearing in June of 1993 in the colours of that carrier. The A310 had arrived at Sharjah on a very hot afternoon in May 1994 and, after a short turn-around, was photographed about to complete its push-back operations in readiness for a departure to Tashkent.

Established in 1992 as the state airline of Azerbaijan, this carrier operates both scheduled and charter passenger and freight services from its base in Baku. The majority of Azerbaijan Airlines' fleet is made up of Soviet-built machines, but Western-manufactured aircraft have now been added which operate to Middle Eastern and European destinations. Azerbaijan's first Boeing 727 arrived at Baku in January 1993 and was photographed at Miami in December 1992 in the final stages of preparation, in fact 4K-4201 left Miami for Baku three days after this picture was taken. The 727 has been re-registered 4K-AZ1 since arriving in the CIS.

Tupolev 154 RA-85713 carries the titles of Alak Airlines, a 1992-formed company based in Moscow. This leasing company has a fleet of five aircraft comprising Tupolev passenger and Ilyushin freight aircraft which provide Aeroflot with additional capacity as and when required. When photographed in September 1995, RA-85713 was about to land at Palma upon the completion of a passenger flight from a Russian destination.

Formerly known as Air Ukraine International, the Kiev-based airline changed its title to Ukraine International Airlines in the summer of 1993 and currently operates international and domestic services with a small fleet of two Boeing 737s. The carrier's international routes brought the Ukraine International colours to the United Kingdom on a twice-weekly service from Kiev to Manchester in the summer of 1993, a service which has since been discontinued. These flights were operated with Boeing 737 400 series equipment and UR-GAA had been selected to perform the service on a Saturday in June 1993 when photographed arriving at Manchester.

(Right top)
This Russian-built Yakovlev 42 is a 120-seat airliner in the service of Air Ukraine, the Kiev-based national carrier of the Ukraine, providing both regional and international passenger and cargo services with a varied fleet of Soviet-built machines. The Yakovlev illustrated here, UR-42377, was constructed in 1989 and was photographed parked between duties at Dubai International Airport in May 1994.

(Right bottom)
One of the carrier's international services is a twice-weekly flight connecting Kiev with North America, and it is at New York's JFK airport where UR-86582, one of seven Ilyushin 62s currently in the fleet, was photographed in May 1993 about to commence its take-off roll upon departure to Kiev.

Aeroflot Russian International Airlines is the international division of the Soviet airline Aeroflot, and the only Russian carrier still officially known by this title. After the break-up of this once vast Soviet carrier into independent airlines, the newly-formed companies gradually applied new titles and liveries to aircraft previously flown in the Aeroflot colour scheme. Ilyushin 76TD RA-76409 is a freighter, and when photographed in May 1994 at Sharjah was still flying in the colours of Aeroflot although at the time the aircraft was part of the fleet of the Moscow-based freight carrier Dobrolet Airlines. This type of aircraft is manufactured in both freight and military versions, each having the navigator's glazed nose section.

Tupolev 154M RA-85681 was at one time an Aeroflot aircraft and flew in those colours until the break-up of the airline. At that time, the newly-formed Moscow Airways applied their own titles and colour scheme and the aircraft entered service providing passenger charter flights from its base at Moscow's Sheremetyevo airport. The Soviet-built tri-jet had brought a tour company's passengers to Dubai when photographed in May 1994.

Included in the fleet of Moscow Airways is an Ilyushin 76TD freighter, which was photographed in May 1994 whilst visiting Sharjah. RA-76498 is a 1982-built machine which also once bore the colours of Aeroflot.

Kyrghyzstan Airlines is another of the newly-formed airlines to emerge since the break-up of Aeroflot. This carrier provides both international and domestic scheduled and charter services with a fleet of Tupolev and Yakovlev aircraft. EX-85519 is one of fourteen Tupolev 154s flown by the carrier which was photographed in May 1994 whilst visiting Sharjah.

Air Georgia was formed in 1992 and operates from Tbilisi, the capital city of the Russian state of Georgia. At the time of writing only one aircraft is in the fleet of Air Georgia, although additional planes are leased as required. A weekly flight from Tbilisi to Germany is provided by the airline and Frankfurt/Main is the location for this August 1995 picture of Tupolev 154B 4L-85547 being pushed back from the gate at the start of its return to Georgia.

Diamond Sakha Airlines is a scheduled international and domestic passenger airline which commenced services in the autumn of 1994 operating out of the Russian Federation city of Sakha Yakutiya. A leased Airbus Industrie A310, previously flown in Pan American colours, was put into service in September of that year appearing in the full colour scheme of the airline, only to fly for the airline for a short period before being returned to the leasing company. The aircraft was then put into storage for a while until reappearing in the same colours operating flights on behalf of the Russian airline Aeroflot. The Airbus has been put into service on Aeroflot's European routes including their Moscow–London service, and it is at London's Heathrow airport that the French registered A310 F-OGYM was photographed in July 1996 arriving on a Saturday flight from the Russian city.

Chapter 3
The Middle East/Africa/West Asia

Nigeria Airways, the flag-carrier of the African state of Nigeria, is owned by the Nigerian government and is based in Lagos. Operations started in 1958 and the airline now provides domestic and international scheduled passenger and cargo services with a fleet of Boeing, Airbus Industrie and McDonnell Douglas airliners. The new livery of the airline introduced in 1993 is seen applied to the carrier's only McDonnell Douglas aircraft, DC-10 5N-ANN, a series 30 model photographed at one of New York JFK airport's remote stands in May 1993, whilst being prepared for a return flight to Africa. Passengers for this flight will be transported to the aircraft by bus from the terminal building.

(Above)
Emirates was established in 1985 as the international airline of the United Arab Emirates and quickly built up a reputation for being the best carrier in the Middle East for quality of service and reliability. The airline is owned 100 per cent by the government of Dubai and it is from this city's airport that the airline provides its comprehensive flights to destinations in Europe, the Far East, Australia and points within the Middle East utilising its young fleet of Airbus Industrie and recently-delivered Boeing 777 airliners. Their first triple seven to be delivered in June 1996 was A6-EMD, which was immediately put into service on the non-stop Dubai–London flights, replacing the Airbus A300 which previously flew the route. The brand-new 777 was photographed in July 1996 about to touchdown on Heathrow's northerly runway at the end of its journey from Dubai.

Iran Air is one of the few worldwide airlines still operating the Boeing 747SP Special Performance airliner. Since being introduced to their fleet in the late 1970s, the carrier has regularly put all of their four examples into service providing flights from Tehran to Turkey, Switzerland, London, Bombay and Austria. Iran Air is government-owned and currently operates an all-jet fleet of Fokker, Airbus Industrie and Boeing aircraft from its Tehran base providing regional and international scheduled and charter passenger and cargo services, the latter flights being handled by Iran Air's pure freighter Boeing 707s. Photographed in August 1993 is one of the airline's SP's EP-IAA about to depart Frankfurt/Main. The airliner is configured 22 business class and 283 economy class and has been in the Iran Air fleet since being delivered new in 1976.

Qatar Amiri Flight Airbus Industrie A340 A7-HHK is a VIP aircraft and operates passenger flights on behalf of the government of Qatar. Upon the completion of crew training, the airline put the A340 into service replacing the operations previously performed by a Boeing 707. The new aircraft now has the distinction of being known as 'Amiri One', a title passed down from the Boeing product. The Airbus was delivered in May 1993 and was photographed making an appearance at Palma in September 1995.

MEA – Middle East Airlines – is the national carrier of the state of Lebanon providing international scheduled passenger and freight services from the country's capital, Beirut. Operations commenced in January 1946, and the carrier's all-jet fleet now consists of Airbus Industrie and Boeing airliners all performing flights within the Middle East, Europe, Africa and the Far East. MEA is one of the few airlines still flying the Boeing 707 in regular passenger service, at the time of writing eight are in the fleet. The 1960s-built airliners are regularly to be observed at airports, and in August 1995 a weekly Sunday flight from Beirut to Germany was diagrammed to be flown by the type. Departing Frankfurt/Main and leaving the showers behind is OD-AGV, a 707 that came out of the Boeing plant in 1968.

Kuwait Airways became known by this title in 1957, prior to which the airline was called Kuwait National Airways following its formation in 1954. The carrier is now government-owned and provides passenger and freight services linking this oil-rich state with major cities in Europe, the USA, Africa and the Far East. A modern all-jet fleet of Boeing and Airbus Industrie aircraft fly to the many destinations served by the airline, and photographed in August 1995 is Airbus A340 9K-AND, the fourth of the type to be delivered to the airline two months earlier. The aircraft had just completed a non-stop flight from Kuwait and is seen approaching its Frankfurt/Main gate.

Frankfurt/Main is also the location for this picture of Egyptair Boeing 737 series 500 SU-GBI photographed about to depart the German city in August 1993. Egyptair is a government-owned airline and commenced operations in 1932, previously being known as United Arab Airlines. The present title was introduced at the end of 1974 and Egyptair's fleet now totals in excess of thirty aircraft manufactured by Boeing and Airbus Industrie. Golf-Bravo-India is one of the shorter fuselage models in the Boeing 737 family and carries the name *Abu Simbel* after the most colossal temple in Egypt, built in the thirteenth century BC by one of the greatest Pharaohs. (The temple, not the 737!)

Chapter 4
India/East Asia

Domestic services within India were, until recently, operated solely by Indian Airlines, the country's only regional scheduled carrier formed in 1953 after the takeover of eight original private airlines. Indian Airlines is one of the world's largest domestic airlines, and until the formation of new regional carriers within the past few years had a monopoly on flights within the country. The first airline to appear in competition was East West Airlines which commenced services in February 1992, a write-up with illustration appeared in the title *Flying Colours* published by Airlife in 1994. Subsequently, a further three airlines started up in competition with the existing airlines, the next one to appear being Jet Airways, which in May 1993 put their newly acquired Boeing 737 series 300s and 400s on flights from its hubs in Bombay, Calcutta and Delhi. At the end of 1995, Jet Airways were providing fifty-two daily flights with an annual seat capacity of 2.37 million. Goa is one of the destinations served, and Boeing 737 VT-JAC, a 300 series aircraft, was photographed a few seconds from touchdown arriving at the resort operating the lunchtime flight from Bombay.

Next to appear was Damania Airways and three leased Boeing 737s were put into service on scheduled flights originating from Bombay. Initial flights were to Bangalore and Goa, and this former Portuguese colony, now a popular Indian holiday resort, is the location for the picture of 737 VT-PDD about to land following its short 1-hour flight from Bombay in February 1995.

(Above)

Within a very short time, yet another domestic carrier appeared on the scene with Modiluft flying an inaugural flight from Bombay to Delhi in May 1993. Again, Boeing 737s were the choice of aircraft and Modiluft took delivery of four examples, leased from the founder Lufthansa. All four 737s which were given the new livery of the Indian airline originally flew in the colours of the German carrier and still carry the names of the German cities applied by Lufthansa. The German livery is still evident as can be seen in the photograph of 737 VT-MGB arriving at Goa in March 1995.

Air Maldives is the national flag-carrier of the Republic of Maldives, a group of atolls situated in the Indian Ocean south-west of Sri Lanka. Its capital is Male and it is in this city that the airline has its base, situated on Hululle Island, a 15-minute boat ride to the north of the capital. To initiate services to the Middle and Far East at the beginning of 1995, the airline leased an Airbus Industrie A300 widebody jet from Malaysian Airways which was turned out in the colours of Air Maldives. The aircraft is also put into service on the four times a week flight to India and it is at the southern state of Kerala's capital city, Trivandrum, that 9M-MHD was photographed in April 1995 about to touchdown upon the completion of the flight from Male.

Air China is the People's Republic of China's national airline and is based in the country's capital, Beijing. Formed in 1949 and originally known as CAAC (Civil Aviation Administration of China), the airline obtained its present title in 1988 after the government of the country formed separate operating divisions, each having its own identity and name. Seattle-built Boeings are the mainstay of Air China's fleet providing services within the mainland with international services linking China to destinations on five continents. Regular flights are made to Australia, and B-2454, a Boeing 747SP of which the airline currently have four examples, was photographed in April 1994 making its way for take-off at Sydney airport. The flying phoenix is the emblem of Air China, symbolising good luck, success and prosperity.

Mandarin Airlines is a subsidiary of the Taiwanese flag-carrier China Airlines and, established in 1991, is now becoming Taiwan's second privately-owned airline. Its small fleet of Boeing and McDonnell Douglas widebody jetliners fly international routes from the country's Chiang Kai Shek Airport linking the Republic of China with Australia and Europe. A twice-weekly service to Germany commenced in the summer of 1995, and McDonnell Douglas MD-11 B-150 was photographed at Frankfurt in August of that year about to depart to Taipei.

Cathay Pacific is the national flag-carrier of Hong Kong and one of the Far East's major airlines flying to more than forty world-wide destinations with an all-jet fleet of Lockheed, Airbus Industrie and Boeing airliners, although at the time of writing, their last remaining seven Lockheed TriStars are due to be taken out of service upon the delivery of further Boeing and Airbus models currently on order. The original colours of Cathay were superseded in August 1994 when their new and current scheme was unveiled upon the delivery of their first Airbus A330. These colours soon began to appear on other airliners in the fleet, one of which being 400 series Boeing 747 VR-HUJ photographed on push-back from Manchester Airport's Terminal 2 in June 1995, about to depart on a one-stop flight to Hong Kong.

(Left bottom)

All Nippon Airways is Japan's largest passenger airline with a fleet of 125 Airbus Industrie and Boeing airliners being put into service on ANA's international and domestic scheduled routes. The airline was established in 1952 and operations commenced towards the end of 1953. Today, All Nippon provide domestic services to over thirty destinations, and their long haul routes take the ANA colours to cities in Asia, Australia, Europe and America. One of the European routes is a thrice-weekly non-stop Tokyo–Frankfurt service, and this flight was photographed in August 1993 upon its arrival at the German city. Boeing 747 JA8174 is a series 200 model and has carried the colours of the airline since being delivered in June 1986.

Japan Airlines, the national airline of Japan, was founded in 1951 and has since built up a vast routeing system providing services to twenty-six countries around the world from its main base at Tokyo. Its current fleet exceeds 100 jet airliners manufactured by Boeing and McDonnell Douglas which are put into service on domestic routes within Japan and long haul services to Europe, the Americas, Australia and the Pacific. Included in the domestic fleet are nine Boeing 747 series 400 aircraft which fly the carrier's short but busy routes, being configured with up to 560 seats. Illustrated is Boeing 747 series 300 which accommodates three classes of travel. The jumbo is carrying the American registration N213JL, and was photographed departing Frankfurt/Main in August 1993.

Chapter 5
Australia/South Pacific

Boeing 747SP VH-EAB, here seen under tow at Sydney Airport in April 1994, carries the titles Australia Asia. Australia Asia Airlines is a wholly-owned subsidiary of the Australian airline Qantas, formed in 1989 to avoid restrictions imposed by the People's Republic of China authorities on carriers that also fly to the Republic of China. These titles were also applied to Boeing 767s, and these aircraft flew exclusively between cities in Australia and Taiwan.

Air New Zealand is the Auckland-based international and domestic airline of New Zealand. Operations started in 1940 as Tasman Empire Airways and it was not until 1965 that the airline's current name was introduced. The present livery appeared in 1973, and is shown on the photograph of Boeing 767 ZK-NCG approaching its allocated gate at Sydney Airport in April 1994. These widebody airliners together with five 747-200s and five 747-400s perform the carrier's long haul routes, whilst Boeing 737s operate the inter-island services.

ZK-NAB, one of Air New Zealand's many 737s, was photographed at Auckland's domestic terminal in March 1994 arriving on an early morning flight from South Island. At the time of writing, the carrier has announced the introduction of a revised livery which will be applied to their fleet.

Air Vanuatu is the state-owned airline of the Republic of Vanuatu, one of the South Pacific's youngest countries. Services started in 1981 linking the capital, Port Vila, with Sydney, and a leased Boeing 737 performed these duties. Non-stop flights operate to Australia and New Zealand, Auckland being served twice a week. Boeing 737 series 400 VH-TJI was originally an Australian Airlines aircraft which passed into the ownership of Qantas upon the merger of the two airlines. When photographed in March 1994 upon its arrival at Auckland it was on lease to Air Vanuatu, and was still flying in the colours of Australian Airlines.

Polynesian Airlines is owned by the government of the independent Polynesian state of Western Samoa and was formed in 1959 to provide a service linking the islands of the South Pacific. Today, the company also provides both passenger and freight services to Australia and New Zealand: its only Boeing 737 being utilised on the latter flights, whilst a Twin Otter and an Islander are employed on short haul inter-island services. The airline's new colour scheme appeared in the summer of 1987 and is seen carried on Boeing 767 C-FMWP, photographed approaching the terminal at Auckland in April 1994. The aircraft was leased to Polynesian from Air Canada from August 1993 until May 1994, being used on services to Los Angeles.

Air Nauru comes from the South Pacific island of the Republic of Nauru and provides regional passenger services with a small fleet of two Boeing 737 400s which entered service with the airline in the summer of 1993 and replaced three 200 series models previously in service. At that time, the airline took the opportunity of introducing their 'new look', which is shown on the photograph of one of the 400s, C2-RN11, about to depart Sydney in April 1994.

Air Caledonie International is a French Polynesian international scheduled and charter passenger airline formed in 1983 and based in Noumea, New Caledonie, a group of islands in the south-west Pacific Ocean. At the time of writing, there are two aircraft in the international fleet: a Twin Otter and a Boeing 737 series 300, the latter flying scheduled services from Noumea to Australia. The Boeing product F-ODGX was making a scheduled arrival at Nadi when photographed in March 1994.

Chapter 6
South America

Aerolineas Argentinas is the national airline of Argentina. Established in 1949, its main base and hub are in the city of Buenos Aires from where its scheduled passenger and cargo services operate. The airline has a comprehensive route network which takes its aircraft to New Zealand, North America and Europe, these services being operated by the carrier's six Boeing 747 series 200 airliners, configured in a three-class layout giving 403 seats. One of their jumbos, LV-MLO, the first of the type to be delivered to the airline in 1979, was captured by the camera arriving at Miami in January 1996 as the sun was just about to set.

Lloyd Aereo Boliviano is the national airline of Bolivia offering both passenger and freight services from its base in Cochabamba. LAB was founded in 1925 and is associated with the Brazilian airline VASP who own shares in the carrier together with the Bolivian government. A Boeing 707 is the carrier's only pure freighter, whilst the rest of the fleet are passenger-carrying airliners, its routes mainly being concentrated within South, Central and North America. A passenger service brings one of the carrier's leased Airbus Industrie A310s to Florida, and CP-2332 was photographed in December 1994 about to touchdown at Miami.

(Opposite top)
McDonnell Douglas DC-8 CC-CAX of Fast Air is a re-engined aircraft and carries the series 71 classification. The aircraft is one of five such DC-8s flown by this Chilean freight carrier based in Santiago de Chile, providing cargo services within North and South America, and Europe. Fast Air has been providing cargo services since its formation in 1972, and at one time Boeing 707s were included in the fleet of freighters. The DC-8 illustrated originally flew as a passenger airliner in the colours of United Air Lines, passing into the Fast Air fleet in 1992. Miami in December 1994 is the location for this photograph.

Aeroperu is the national flag-carrier of Peru, the third largest country in South America, renowned as the land of the Incas. The airline's base is in Lima from where its small fleet of Boeing airliners provides national and international flights. Aeroperu is a member of the Aeromexico Group and from time to time leases aircraft from the group to operate its services. In December 1994, the daily Lima–Miami service was being operated by a leased Boeing 757, XA-SMD, which appeared with Aeroperu titles having previously flown in the colours of Aeromonterrey, a Mexican airline that folded several weeks earlier.

Brazil's principal airline is Varig, founded in 1927 as the first airline in Brazil. An extensive route network within Brazil, Central and North America, Europe and Asia is provided utilising a modern fleet of jetliners manufactured by Boeing and McDonnell Douglas. The airline currently fly ten Boeing 767 extended-range models which entered service in 1987 and are used on their Fortaleza–Miami service. PP-VNR was the 767 used on this service when photographed in January 1996 about to touch-down at the Florida resort.

Trans Brasil is Brazil's third largest airline and is based in São Paulo. Formed in 1955 as a carrier of meat, the airline was known as Sadia SA Transportes Aereos until 1972 when the present title Transbrasil Linhas Aereas was adopted. Today, the airline provides both passenger and cargo scheduled and charter flights with an all-Boeing aircraft fleet. European services from Rio de Janeiro and São Paulo take the Trans Brasil colours to Amsterdam and Vienna, whilst their extended-range models also make regular flights to Miami. One of the members of the fleet is PP-TAI which was photographed in December 1994 making an early morning departure from Miami.

(Previous page)
Avianca Airlines recently celebrated its seventy-fifth anniversary. Commencing passenger services in 1920 from the Colombian city Barranquilla, the airline flew a varied selection of propeller-driven aircraft including the Douglas DC-3 and Lockheed Constellation, mainly in and around Colombia. It was in 1946 that Avianca expanded its services to become an international carrier upon the introduction of flights to Miami and New York, and upon leasing a Boeing 707 in 1960, the airline became the first company in Latin America to provide a jet service. Avianca's current fleet consists of Fokker, McDonnell Douglas and Boeing aircraft, the majority carrying the warm red livery of the airline. Boeing 757 N989AN, photographed in December 1994 a few feet from touchdown at Miami, wears an all-white scheme during a period of lease to the carrier.

(Opposite top)
Servivensa is a subsidiary of the Venezuelan airline Avensa, and operates from the country's capital Caracas with a fleet of McDonnell Douglas and Boeing aircraft, used on their regional and domestic passenger services. The airline provides thrice-daily round trip flights between Caracas and Miami, the last flight of the day to Venezuela being their 17.45 departure from Miami. Boeing 727 YV-843C was operating this flight to the country's Simon Bolivar Airport when photographed at sunset in December 1995.

(Opposite bottom)
Aces Colombia (Aerolineas Centrales de Colombia) commenced operations in 1972 operating extensive passenger services within Colombia from hubs in Bogotá, Medellín and Cali. These services are operated by the carrier's de Havilland Twin Otters flying to more than three dozen destinations within the country. International charter flights started soon after, to be followed in the summer of 1992 by a North American service with which the airline introduced the Boeing 727 to its fleet. Currently, there are eight examples of the type in the company colours. Aces operates two return non-stop flights a day to Miami, one from Bogotá, the other from Medellín, each arriving and departing within 40 minutes of each other. Boeing 727 HK-3977-X, photographed at Miami in December 1994, is configured all business class travel.

Tampa Colombia is purely a freight airline based in Medellín flying a fleet of Boeing 707s and McDonnell Douglas DC-8s, the latter aircraft having been re-engined and re-classified DC-8 series 71F. The company was formed in 1973 and operates regularly between Colombia, North America and the Caribbean. The original livery of the airline was modified in the summer of 1987 and is illustrated in the shot of one of their Boeing 707s coming into Miami in January 1995.

Chapter 7
Central America/Mexico

Following the demise of the Nicaraguan airline Aeronica, the government of this central American country formed NICA, (Nicaraguenses de Aviacion), and commenced services in the summer of 1992 with daily scheduled flights from Managua to Miami. Boeing 737 N501NG is the company's only jetliner, and operates this service. The twin-jet was photographed in December 1995 as it approaches Miami after completing the journey from Nicaragua, and after a short stay will return to Nicaragua, to re-appear tomorrow. The other aircraft in this airline's fleet is currently a Casa 212 24-seat aircraft which connects Managua with other destinations within the country.

APA International Air, whilst being a Dominican Republic airline, is actually based in Miami, Florida. The airline was founded in 1980 to provide international, regional and domestic services from the Dominican airports Santo Domingo and Puerto Plata to North America. The Peruvian airline Faucett provides the aircraft on a wet-leased basis which are flown in the full colours of APA International. When photographed in January 1996, Airbus Industrie A300 OB-1611 was a new aircraft to have joined the Faucett fleet, and was on lease to APA when operating a flight into Miami. Previously, APA colours had been applied to Lockheed L1011 aircraft which have also made regular appearances in the USA.

Aero Costa Rica commenced flying in the spring of 1992 with flights between the airline's base at San Jose and Miami using two Boeing 727s previously flown by Eastern Airlines and Pan American. These two airliners continued in service with the company started by former employees of Lacsa, Costa Rica's national carrier, until being replaced by two Boeing 737s in late summer 1993. Photographed at Miami in December 1994 is 737 N171PL which is no longer flying in Aero Costa Rica colours, having been acquired by Halisa Air and illustrated opposite. The Boeing twin-jets are no longer in the fleet of the Costa Rican carrier which in April 1996 reverted to providing services with Boeing 727s.

New to the airways in 1995 was Halisa Air – Les Ailes d'Haiti – commencing services in April with flights between Port-au-Prince and Fort Lauderdale, Florida, later including Miami to their schedule. A Boeing 737 was put into service on this 700-mile route, the twin-jet being allocated 2 hours to complete the journey. At this time, only one aircraft carries the Halisa colours, shown here on N171PL arriving on one of the airline's flights to Miami in December 1995. Prior to entering service with Halisa, this aircraft flew for Aero Costa Rica, joining that carrier after a period flying for the Asian airline Dragonair.

Allegro Air, one of Mexico's national and international charter airlines is based in Monterrey, and commenced services in December 1992 upon the acquisition of two Boeing 727s. The airline's fleet has since been enlarged and now includes McDonnell Douglas DC-9 and MD-83 airliners. Boeing 727 XA-SXO was the first of the two Boeings to be put into service by Allegro, and the 167-seat tri-jet was photographed in May 1995 about to depart Cancun with returning holidaymakers to a North American destination.

Aviacsa was founded in 1990 and originally operated routes in Mexico's Yucatán district with two leased BAe 146 aircraft. At that time its base was at Tuxtla Gutiérrez, the state of Chiapas' capital city. In 1992, the 146s were replaced with Fokker 100s and services expanded to include other destinations including Monterrey and Mexico City. Aviacsa is now owned by AeroExo, the Monterrey-based airline that purchased the carrier in 1994, although Aviacsa still operates as a separate company. Since being under new ownership, Boeing 727s originally carrying the AeroExo titles have been added to the fleet. Only the Fokker 100s carry names and the picture is of XA-SBH bearing the name *Uxmal* after the archaeological site situated in the Yucatán. The jet is seen about to come to a halt at Mexico City Airport in July 1992.

Taesa commenced scheduled services in 1991 from its Mexico City base and has since risen to become the third largest airline in Mexico with a fleet in excess of forty aircraft. The airline operates both domestic and international services to cities in Mexico and the United States, and to more than sixty other worldwide desti-nations. McDonnell Douglas DC-9 XA-SXT joined the Taesa fleet in 1995 and is an 85-seat series 15 model which previously flew in the colours of British Midland Airways. Photographed at Merida in June of that year, the aircraft will remain on the ground for 45 minutes before returning on the 90-minute flight to Mexico City.

Aero California was established in 1982 and is based at La Paz, the capital city of Baja California, the world's longest peninsula situated at the tip of southern California. The whole of the carrier's fleet consists of McDonnell Douglas DC-9 series 14 and 15 aircraft which operate within Mexico and southern California. A comprehensive service operates from various destinations to Mexico City, and it is at this airport that XA-AGS, a series 15 model, was photographed in May 1995.

Chapter 8
The Caribbean

Regional air services commenced in 1988 and Air Aruba later began international services, the first of which was in 1990 to Miami. Based on the Dutch Caribbean island of Aruba, this national flag-carrier now operates a fleet of McDonnell Douglas DC-9 and MD-83/88 airliners with daily services still operating on the Aruba–Miami route. MD-83s are normally put into service on these flights and when photographed in December 1995, P4-MDE was the aircraft chosen.

Following the privatisation of the airline, Air Jamaica launched a marketing campaign entitled 'Spirit of Jamaica' and applied a new colourful livery to one of their Boeing 727s. Scheduled passenger and cargo services are provided by the airline whose base is in Kingston, capital city of Jamaica. Together with Boeing 727s, the airline operates Airbus Industrie aircraft on services from Kingston and Montego Bay to other Caribbean Islands and mainland USA. A frequent service is provided between Kingston and Miami, and it is at this Florida city that Boeing 727 6Y-JMO was photographed in January 1996 resplendent in its newly acquired livery. The new colours will be applied to the whole of Air Jamaica's fleet as aircraft become due for re-painting.

Chapter 9
North America/Canada

American Trans Air was founded in 1973 and is now the largest charter airline in the United States. Based in the Indiana city of Indianapolis, the airline's fifty-plus fleet of Boeing and Lockheed aircraft provides charter flights within the USA together with services to Europe. At the beginning of 1994 a new charter programme was initiated with Pleasant Hawaiian Holidays, a company operating tours to this fiftieth state of the USA. Two dedicated Lockheed L1011s were painted with Pleasant Hawaiian titles replacing the American Trans Air titles. One of these airliners is N191AT, which was photographed in December 1995 about to touchdown at Miami.

Based in Columbia, South Carolina, Air South began scheduled operations in August 1994 with flights from Columbia to Atlanta, and has since built up its routes to include several cities in Florida, South Carolina and Georgia. Air South's fleet consists entirely of all-coach configured Boeing 737s leased from various leasing companies. EI-CKW is one of the carrier's aircraft which is leased from Polaris, and was photographed in December 1994 approaching Miami on an afternoon service from Atlanta.

American Trans Air shortened its titles and unveiled a completely new livery in November 1994 to present itself as the leader in the charter market. A Boeing 757 was the first of the company's airliners to receive the new scheme, and it was not too long before other aircraft in the fleet appeared in the brightly painted livery. Boeing 727 N755US illustrates the new scheme photographed on push-back at the Mexican resort of Cancun in May 1995, just at the end of a tropical storm.

ValuJet commenced operations in October 1993 with a small fleet of McDonnell Douglas series 32 DC-9s. The Atlanta-based company intended to compete with airlines already flying the same routes, with much lower fares but without the frills. Tickets are dispensed with as are crew uniforms, and the whole formality normally experienced with air travel is not to be seen. No meal service – merely peanuts and pretzels! ValuJet have built up a comprehensive route system with new cities being added on a regular basis, their DC-9s flying to destinations in direct competition with Delta, from whom their aircraft were purchased. First and Business Classes are not available on ValuJet, their DC-9s being operated in an all-coach configuration. N1269L is one of the company's series 32 models and has since been re-registered as N911VV, having been delivered new to Delta Airlines in 1968, and remaining in service with them until 1994. ValuJet's colours incorporate their unique logo, known as 'Critter', which is also their call-sign, and this picture was taken in December 1994 as the aircraft was about to depart on a morning service out of Fort Lauderdale. Since preparing this text, ValuJet have been grounded for several months following their fatal accident in the Florida Everglades and services have recommenced on a very much reduced scale.

(Previous page top)
Boeing 737 N206AU is part of the fleet of Carnival Air Lines, the Fort Lauderdale-based company in Florida. This airliner is permanently in the colours of the Miami Basketball team which was recently purchased by the owners of Carnival Air Lines, and is used to transport team members to away games. Photographed at its Fort Lauderdale base in December 1994, the aircraft, *Miami Heat*, is awaiting its next assignment.

(Previous page bottom)
Miami Air was one of several new US airlines to appear in 1991, formed as Miami Air International, a privately-owned charter airline based in Miami offering services to the Caribbean, North and South America. Operations commenced with flights to Havana, Cuba, initially with two Boeing 727s. There are now five examples of this aircraft in the Miami Air fleet, all being configured Economy Class, each with 173 seats. One aircraft carries the name *Lois*, and once flew for the American airline Eastern before joining its current owner and being re-registered as N804MA. *Lois* was photographed at Miami in January 1996 about to depart on a late afternoon/early evening flight.

(Left)
Ten years after the fall of his airline, Sir Freddie re-started Laker Airways in May 1992 with flights between Fort Lauderdale, Florida, and Freeport. The services originated as charter flights later to become scheduled operations in December of that year, when additional routes were also introduced. Two 1973-built Boeing 727s, previously flown by the Danish airline Sterling and Mexican airline Mexicana, currently operate the Laker North American services, and N553NA was photographed in December 1994 about to depart Fort Lauderdale on the 09.00 flight to Freeport.

For a number of years, Freddie Laker has publicly let it be known that he was anxious to reintroduce his transatlantic flights, which became a reality in the spring of 1996 when charter flights commenced on the Manchester–Orlando route. McDonnell Douglas DC-10s were again the Laker choice for long haul services of which the airline now have three in the fleet. N833LA is one of the series 30 'tens' to carry the Laker name and colours which is configured full Economy Class with 353 seats, and was photographed in July 1996 as the tow truck slowly brings it to its Manchester Terminal 2 gate to be prepared to receive passengers for Orlando.

Miami's Freighters

Kalitta American International Airways' main base and hub is at Willow Run Airport, Ypsilanti, Michigan, from where it provides scheduled and charter, passenger and cargo services. The airline was originally known as Connie Kalitta Services, named after its president Connie Kalitta, with the present title becoming effective in March 1991. The basic livery was not altered at that time but the titles began to be replaced with the airline's new name, 'Kalitta' at first, then with the additional 'American International Airlines' at a later date. Kalitta's fleet is predominantly cargo-carrying although eight aircraft are passenger configured and leased out to other airlines as required. Boeing 747 N701CK, photographed whilst parked at Miami in December 1994, was originally a passenger-carrying aircraft in the fleet of Japan Airlines, being converted to a freighter in 1992.

Millon Air is an international, regional and domestic cargo airline, and was established in 1983 having its main base and hub at Miami. Millon's routes are mainly to Latin America with Ecuador being one of the main destinations. There are currently six aircraft in the company's fleet: five Boeing 707s and one Lockheed L1011, the latter having joined the airline in the summer of 1996. Boeing 707 N751MA photographed in the final stages of landing at Miami in December 1993, carries the name *Vanessa*. The 1967-built aircraft entered service during that year as a passenger-carrying airliner with American Airlines, and received the Millon Air colours upon entering service with the freighter at the end of 1989.

Fine Air is another of Miami's freight-carrying airlines having been established in 1992. This carrier specialises in scheduled and charter cargo flights to destinations in the Caribbean and Latin America with a fleet made up entirely of McDonnell Douglas DC-8s. Illustrated is N54FA about to touchdown on Miami's 9R runway in January 1996 and considering this aircraft is almost 35 years old, it certainly appears to be in good external condition.

Trans Continental is a subsidiary of Kalitta American International and shares its headquarters in Michigan. Operations commenced in August 1994 providing similar services to the parent company with McDonnell Douglas DC-8 equipment. Flights are made to destinations in South America, and at the time of preparing this book, the company's fleet stands at four. Photographed about to land on Miami's southernmost runway in January 1996 is N803MG, a 1967-built aircraft from the McDonnell Douglas factory which started life as a passenger-carrying airliner for the Italian carrier Alitalia.

(Left bottom)
North America has a vast number of air cargo carriers, as the distances involved make it unrealistic for goods to be carried any other way but by air. Miami airport accommodates many of these airlines with large areas surrounding the international airport being set aside for the construction of warehouses and loading bays. One such area is devoted for the use of Southern Air Transport, a Columbus, Ohio, charter cargo carrier, and members of the airline's fleet can be regularly observed preparing for flight. Southern Air started operations in 1947 and now have an impressive fleet of over twenty freighters. Boeing 747 N740SJ is one of four jumbos flown by the company after being converted from passenger-carrying airliners, and was photographed whilst parked in the carrier's 'parking lot' at Miami in December 1994.

Atlas Air is one of the newcomers to the North American freight scene being established in 1992. Their main base and hub is at New York City's JFK airport from where airport-to-airport worldwide transportation is made together with their existing round the world westbound service New York–Hong Kong–New York. The entire fleet of Atlas Air is made up of Boeing 747s, currently totalling sixteen examples one of which being N509MC, having received the Atlas colours in the spring of 1995 after serving almost twenty years flying for the German airline Lufthansa as a passenger carrier. Miami is again the location for this December 1995 photograph.

Western Pacific Airlines began service on 28 April 1995 with flights to five cities and have since built up a route system which offers travellers non-stop service to nineteen cities from their base in Colorado Springs, Colorado. The airline currently has fourteen aircraft and surely must claim to have more flying colours than any other commercial airline in the world. The author was fortunate to be a guest of the airline during August 1996 and had the opportunity to photograph their whole fleet of Boeing 737 series 300 airliners. Western Pacific received national and international attention in the summer of 1995 from its 'Air Logo' programme in which advertising space on the exterior of their single class 138-seat planes was sold. Not all aircraft carry advertising material at this time, but those still in Western Pacific colours also provide various schemes. It is the company's intention to secure new clients for their successful advertising programme, with new designs being applied to additional aircraft which are due to be put into service shortly.

First of the aircraft to appear bearing advertising was N947WP, which emerged from the paint shop carrying the Broadmoor Hotel markings, a five-star property resort located in Colorado Springs. The owner of the hotel is an investor in the airline.

Number four was rolled out in the summer of 1995, and the City of Colorado Springs was the sponsor. The opportunity to promote the city was given to N951WP.

(Right)
Flying Billboards numbers five and six appeared simultaneously in November 1995, with N950WP receiving the colours of the Las Vegas-based Stardust Casino, complete with reproductions of a showgirl on each side of the tail, and N961WP which is sponsored by the Thrifty Car Rental Company, the official Car Rental Company of Western Pacific.

When number eight made its appearance the sponsor was the San Antonio-based Security Service Federal Credit Union, which is also in fact the official credit union of the airline. N948WP entered service with the carrier in these colours in April 1996.

The airline continued to promote their advertising facilities, and the seventh sponsor to take up this opportunity in March 1996 was the Professional Rodeo Cowboys Association. N375TA carries the bright red colours of this organisation, with ProRodeo Hall of Fame titles appearing on one side and Professional Rodeo Cowboys on the other side. On each side of the tail there are images of riding cowboys.

At the time of writing, the last fully painted airliner in sponsorship colours is N955WP, which is promoting the Boyd Gaming Corporation's Sam's Town Hotel and Gambling Hall in the Nevada city, Las Vegas.

Another 737 with a similar scheme to N960WP is N945WP, which carries a red and blue livery on one side of the aircraft. The same design is repeated on the port side of this 737 with the colours being reversed.

(Opposite top)
It is expected that two more 737s will promote other Sam's Towns in Kansas City and Tunica, Mississippi, and N956WP will be one of the aircraft repainted to sponsor these resorts in the near future.

(Opposite bottom)
Western Pacific aircraft still fly in various house colour schemes pending sponsorships, and N960WP is illustrated in one of the carrier's own billboard schemes.

N509AU was delivered to the airline in November 1995 after serving in the fleet of US Air. The WP markings and metallic finish are provisional, and for the present period the airliner will carry the cartoon character 'WestPac Willie'. It is expected that the aircraft will be re-registered N953WP in the near future.

(Opposite bottom)
Finally, N962WP is promoting the airline's own special summer saver fares. These titles were added specially for the summer period, replacing previous promotions 'Winter Wonderland' (complete with sleigh) and Spring Fling Jet titles carried earlier in the year.

AirTran Airways was known, until August 1994, as Conquest Sun Airlines, a 1993-formed, Fort Lauderdale-based company operating a single Boeing 737. Upon the name change, the airline enlarged its fleet when additional 737s were put into service, also at that time the company's base moved further north in the state of Florida to its present location in Orlando. AirTran Airways is a scheduled passenger-carrying airline offering services to ten North American cities, currently with a fleet of seven series 200 Boeing 737s. One of these services in August 1996 was a daily round trip non-stop between Orlando and Kansas City and N737Q was the aircraft operating this flight when photographed at Kansas City about to return to Orlando. This is an early morning departure, the inbound flight having arrived the night before.

Air Transat is a Canadian international scheduled and charter passenger airline operating out of Montreal International Airport. The company was established in 1986 and provides services to a number of destinations in the Americas, Europe and the Caribbean with an all-jet fleet of economy class-configured Boeing and Lockheed airliners. One of the carrier's Lockheed L1011 TriStars is the 1972-built C-FTNA which entered service with Air Transat in 1988 after previously flying in the colours of Eastern Airlines, and was photographed in July 1995 arriving at Manchester after an overnight flight from Canada.

(Opposite bottom)
Canada's second largest airline is Canadian Airlines International which was founded at the beginning of 1988, a result of the merger between Pacific Western and Canadian Pacific Airlines. The present fleet consists of approximately eighty aircraft manufactured by Airbus Industrie, Boeing and McDonnell Douglas providing services to over 150 worldwide destinations. The German city of Frankfurt/Main is one of their European destinations, and photographed at that city in August 1995 was McDonnell Douglas DC-10 C-FCRE just about ready and secure to depart to Canada. This series 30 aircraft carries the signatures of the company's employees who entered a 'name the aircraft' contest.

Air Canada is the country's largest airline both in terms of employees and aircraft, and has been operating services since its formation in 1937. International, regional and domestic services are provided from various hubs in Canada to destinations in the USA, Europe and Asia, together with at least sixty internal points within Canada. Services to these cities are provided by the airline's comprehensive fleet of aircraft which include McDonnell Douglas, Boeing, Airbus Industrie, Lockheed and the recently delivered Canadair Regional Jet 100 domestic airliner. The new livery of Air Canada, replacing the former red and white scheme which had been in use since 1977, appeared in December 1993 and is shown in the picture of Boeing 767 C-FVNM photographed in August 1995 departing Manchester on the carrier's daily flight to Toronto.

(Top)
Royal Airlines commenced operations in
April 1992 as an international and regional
charter airline providing services to various points in Canada, the USA, Europe and
the Caribbean. The carrier's main base is
Montreal from where their fleet of Boeing
727s and Lockheed L1011s are put into service on charter traffic. Northern hemi-
sphere winter services to Florida are
included in Royal's schedules with regular
flights to Fort Lauderdale being operated
by 727s, and it is at this location that
C-FRYS was photographed in December
1994 about to return to Canada. This 727 is
one of only a small number of the type to
be fitted with winglets.

Airbus Industrie A320 C-GVXB is one of
five of the type flown by Canada 3000, a
Toronto-based charter passenger airline.
Services commenced in 1988 as Air 2000
Airlines, a company partially owned by the
United Kingdom Travel Group Owners
Abroad. This organisation is the parent
company of the UK airline Air 2000 which
accounts for the fact that both airline liver-
ies are identical. Boeing 757s are also

included in the Canada 3000 fleet which
are often leased from the British airline
during the UK's quieter periods, the Air
2000 titles being simply replaced by those
of the Canadian airline. The Airbus illustrated commenced flying in these colours
in the summer of 1993 and was photographed on departure from Fort
Lauderdale in December of that year.